GIRL EATS GOOD

Hearty, Nourishing, and Stress-free Recipes

by Jo Kenny

KINGSLEY
PUBLISHERS

First published in South Africa by Kingsley Publishers, 2023
Copyright © Jo Kenny, 2023

*The right of Jo Kenny to be identified as author of
this work has been asserted.*

*Kingsley Publishers
Pretoria, South Africa
www.kingsleypublishers.com*

*A catalogue copy of this book will be available from the National Library of South Africa
Hardcover ISBN: 978-1-7764317-5-5
Paperback ISBN: 978-1-7764317-6-2
eBook ISBN: 978-1-7764317-7-9*

*All rights reserved. No part of this publication may be reproduced, stored in a retrieval system
or transmitted, in any form or by any means, electronic, mechanical, photocopying, recording or
otherwise, without the prior written permission of the publisher.*

Also by Jo Kenny

Cook it Eat it Live it

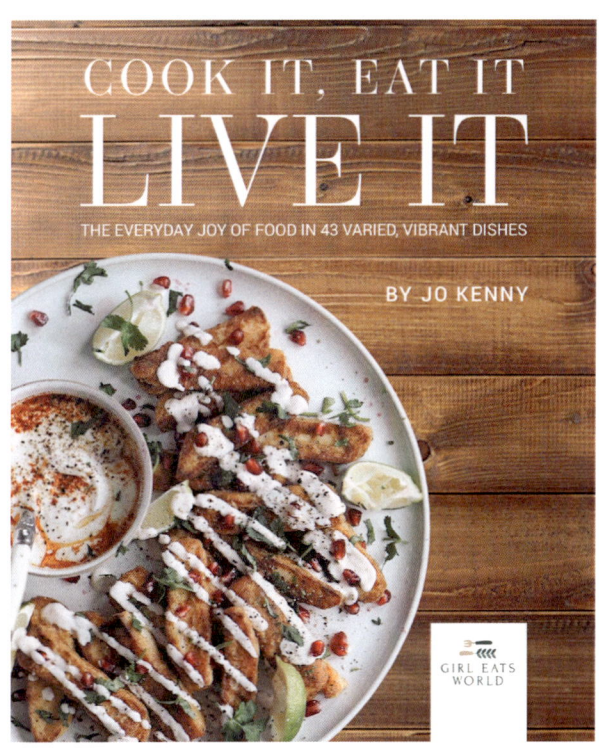

For my son Callum, who sparks endless excitement
in me for all our adventures ahead!
We are going to have so much fun.

Introduction

Well, here we are - book number two! Oh, if I could go back in time to when I began the cookbook journey and tell myself that we would be here… I would love to see my face. Although, I suppose my reaction would be just the same as it is presently - one great big, happy smile. I have absolutely loved this journey, and to see book number two manifested is a dream come true. But even more than this - thank you for joining me, and I really hope that you love this next series of delicious recipes for your home.

My first book 'Cook It, Eat It, Live It' felt like a really personal introduction to me and my cooking style. I spoke about my inspirations, my philosophy around food, and shared all the dishes that I cook regularly in my own home. I spoke about my passion for hearty, wholesome food, and how I love to inject everyday joy into my life through cooking. Life after all, is only sprinkled with wow-factor moments, and for the most part it is made up of regular, routine activities. Cooking is one of them. But routine doesn't have to be mundane, and I believe that harnessing good food is the perfect way to practise frequent, happy moments in your life.

Joyful food continues to be the inspiration for my next book, partnered thoughtfully with what feels like an inescapable reflection over the last few years. I think it is fair to say that we have all been through a lot since 2020. We have all been challenged in ways that we never could have imagined. Not too long ago, my husband Alex told me he doesn't think we truly yet grasp how the pandemic has affected us all, because we are still so close to it. Only in years to come, when lockdowns are a hazy memory and pandemic buzzwords have long gone unused, will we look back and fathom the magnitude of what we all lived through. It has been a momentous segment of our lives and I don't think anyone has come out on the other side unchanged. I certainly haven't.

For me, living through a pandemic came with the added challenge of a pregnancy, and this brought about its extra share of physical and mental difficulties. They say that having a child can spark you to reassess your priorities, and sure enough, with the seismic global changes and my own personal circumstances to boot, I found myself reflecting more than ever on the importance of wellbeing, and how to preserve it.

When you start to delve into it, it is an incredibly interesting subject. If you asked a room full of people what wellbeing meant to them, I am willing to bet that you would not get a single matching answer. We are, of course, all wonderfully different with unique interests and motivations. Whichever way we achieve wellbeing for ourselves, wellbeing should, at least according to the Oxford dictionary, 'bring about a sense of comfort, health, and happiness'. And if I may circle back to my mantra on the joy of food - happiness is what 'Girl Eats World' is all about.

We've all got to eat, so the last thing cooking should feel like is a chore. A common complaint I always hear from followers on social media is the difficulty of coming up with ideas for dinner, every day, for the rest of your life.

I can't help but chuckle, because when you put it like that it sounds undeniably daunting! There is nothing worse than staring into the depths of your cupboards and coming up with blanks. Viewing mealtimes as an eternal burden surely cannot be good for your wellbeing. Neither is losing inspiration and reaching for the cereal box again. Food itself should be joyful, and the process of getting it onto your plate should be stress-free.

So, with all this in mind, I wanted my next book to be a real celebration of fresh ingredients, as components of effortless meals that maximise those good feelings. You will find wonderful everyday recipes to navigate you through breakfast, lunch, dinner, and snacks. Your time is precious, so there are loads of speedy meals to keep you eating well, even when life gets hectic. I hope that this collection of recipes delights your taste buds, while removing the 'Oh God, what shall we eat today' drama from your life.

A big part of wellbeing starts in the kitchen, so let's keep it stress-free and exciting.

Happy Cooking!

Contents

BREAKFAST

15 Coconut Crepes
16 Fruit and Nut Muffins
19 Banana Pancake Bites
20 Apple Crisp
23 Orange and Cranberry Granola
24 Breakfast Bruschetta with Basil and Spinach Pesto
27 Strawberry Baked Oats
28 Spiced Apple and Raisin Bircher

SOUPS

33 Curried Parsnip Soup
34 Pea and Asparagus Soup
37 Creamy Red Pepper and Basil Soup
38 Carrot and Ginger Soup
41 Creamy Spinach and Orzo Soup
42 Spicy Sweet Potato Soup

SALADS

47 Cheese Crunch Lettuce Cups
48 Goats Cheese and Apple Salad
51 Mango Couscous Salad
52 Avocado and Black Bean Chopped Salad
55 Grilled Peaches with Burrata and Mint
56 Chickpea Garden Salad with Honey Mustard Dressing
59 Creamy Cucumber and Chinese Cabbage with Dill
61 Courgette and Lentil Salad with Caramelised Onions
62 Greek Style Salad with Chunky Croutons
65 Warm Kale, Sweet Potato and Apple Salad

VEGGIES

68 Charred Balsamic Sprouts
71 Honey Miso Glazed Aubergines
72 Sesame Roasted Broccoli and Courgettes

75   Sticky Carrot and Courgette Ribbons

76   Creamy Minted Root Veg and Peas

79   Kale with Caramelised Walnuts

80   Spinach and Cauliflower Blue Cheese

83   Charred Corn with Smoked Paprika Butter

LIGHT BITES

87   Red Pepper and Basil Pasta

88   Mediterranean Vegetable Tart

91   Sweet Fried Plantain and Feta Tacos

92   Creamy Spinach Stuffed Mushrooms

95   Couscous with Slow Roasted Tomatoes and Parmesan

96   Cavolo Nero Spaghetti with Garlic and Lemon

99   Roasted Vegetable Orzo

100   Broccoli Pasta

103   Courgette Fritters with Lemon Yoghurt

SNACKS

106   Pear and Ginger Cakes

109   Date and Cashew Bars

110   Sweet and Spicy Roasted Chickpeas

113   Courgette Scones

114   Rustic Oatcakes

117   Carrot and Orange Loaf

118   Creamy Spinach Pinwheels

DIPS AND DRESSINGS

123   Garlic Sauce

123   Green Sauce

124   Sweet Garlic and Thyme Dressing

124   The Perfect Guac

127   Sweet Onion Dip

127   Whipped Feta with Spiced Chickpeas

128   Peanut Dressing

128   Spiced Honey

130   Ginger, Honey and Lime Dressing

COOKING NOTES

Oven Temperatures

All temperatures stated are intended for use with a fan oven. If your oven is not fan-assisted, please add 20c to the temperature in the recipe.

Measure with your heart

Your food is all about... you! The fun of cooking is being creative and in control of your meals. So, if you fancy a bit more cheese, you grate away. If you want a handful of herbs to be a little bigger or smaller, then go right ahead. Salt and pepper are a given, so they are not noted in recipes. Again, you are in control of adding to taste.

For across the pond

As a UK cook, I measure in metric. But here is a handy conversion chart for those who might need it (numbers are rounded for easy reference, we are keeping this stress-free after all!)

Cups	Grams	ml
1/4	30g	60ml
1/3	40g	80ml
1/2	65g	120ml
2/3	85g	160ml
3/4	95g	180ml
1	125g	240ml
1 ¼	155g	300ml
1 ⅓	165g	230ml
1 ½	190g	350ml
1 ⅔	210g	390ml
1 ¾	220g	420ml
2	250g	470ml

BREAKFAST

Wake up those tastebuds! I couldn't care less about the debate regarding whether breakfast is the most important meal of the day, or not - because it's important to me. I love breakfast. Anyway, who wants to be hangry until lunch time - so here we have some delicious recipes to satisfy both the sweet-tooths and the savoury lovers. There are some lovely breakfasts to enjoy at the table, over weekends, and a few tasty-yet-filling bites for on the go.

Coconut Crepes

Prep time: 2 mins   **Cooking time: 8 mins**   **Serves: 2**

These are gorgeously silky pancakes with a creamy hit of coconut flavour. They work fantastically with both sweet and savoury toppings.

Ingredients

- 170g plain flour
- Pinch of salt
- 1 can coconut milk
- 2 eggs, beaten

Method

In a bowl add the flour and salt, then pour in the coconut milk slowly, while whisking. Now whisk in the beaten egg until you have a smooth batter.

Lightly grease a frying pan and heat it on low-medium heat. Add about three-quarters of a ladle of pancake mix to the pan at a time. Tilt and rotate the frying pan so the pancake mix spreads evenly across the base of the pan to form a uniform round crepe. Cook for 1 minute, then flip and cook for a further minute.

Use a spatula to fold the pancake into half, and half again, then add to a plate and keep warm in the oven while you repeat the process. Top with whatever you fancy - I love raspberries and honey.

Fruit and Nut Muffins

Prep time: 10 mins   Cooking time: 20 mins   Serves: 8

Packed with texture and filling ingredients, these delicious and ultra-rustic muffins will keep you going all morning. Bake a batch on the weekend, ready for those on-the-go breakfasts, perfect for the busy week ahead.

Ingredients

- 5 ripe bananas, mashed
- 4 tbsp olive oil
- 5 tbsp honey
- Pinch of salt
- 130g whole oats
- 100g dried cranberries, chopped
- 100g pecans, chopped
- 100g sunflower seeds
- Zest and juice of 1 orange

Method

Preheat your oven to 170c.

In a bowl, add the mashed bananas, olive oil, honey and salt. Give these a thorough mix until combined.

Now mix in the oats, cranberries, pecans, sunflower seeds, the orange juice, and zest.

Spoon into greased muffin moulds and bake for 20 minutes.

Banana Pancake Bites

Prep time: 5 mins   Cooking time: 10 mins   Serves: 2

These are so much fun for all ages. I challenge anyone not to feel cheerful after starting their day with these little delights!

Ingredients

- 2 bananas, sliced into 1cm disks
- 100g self-raising flour
- 1 tbsp baking powder
- 1.5 tsp cinnamon
- 1 tsp ground ginger
- 200ml milk

Method

To a bowl, add flour, baking powder, cinnamon, and ginger. Slowly pour in the milk, while whisking, until all the milk is poured in. Keep whisking until your batter is smooth.

Now tip in your banana slices and carefully stir until they're all well coated.

Heat up your frying pan on low-medium heat and add a little butter or oil to the pan - just enough to grease.

Take pieces of the battered banana slices and add to the pan, spacing evenly.

The banana pancakes should be ready to flip in 60 seconds, or when they look a rich golden brown on the underside. Use a spatula or fork to turn them over.

Repeat until all the banana pancakes are cooked. You can keep those that are already cooked warm in the oven at 50c.

Serve with honey, fresh fruit, or yoghurt. Or why not all three?

Apple Crisp

Prep time: 5 mins   Cooking time: 5 mins   Serves: 2

These are sweet, chewy, warming, and most importantly - filling! For me there is nothing worse than finishing breakfast, only to realise that you're still peckish. This is a proper start to the day.

Ingredients

- 150ml water
- 3 tbsp honey
- 1 tsp cinnamon
- ½ tsp ground ginger
- 2 apples, cut into thin wedges
- 2 handfuls of oats
- 4 tbsp Greek yoghurt

Method

In a pan, on medium heat, add the water, honey, cinnamon, and ginger. Stir until warmed, to create a sticky sauce. Then add the apples and cook until they have softened. Now add the oats and warm through.

Serve in bowls with a dollop of Greek yoghurt.

Orange and Cranberry Granola

Prep time: 5 mins   **Cooking time: 25 mins**   **Serves: 6**

A celebration of natural sweetness and crunchy textures. Granola is just a joy to eat! This recipe will have your house smelling incredible too. Make in advance and store it in airtight jars. Ready for a pouring of milk, sprinkling over yoghurt or just on its own as a snack.

Ingredients

- 250g rolled oats
- Zest of 1 orange
- 100g dried cranberries
- 100ml honey
- 1 tsp ginger
- 1 tsp cinnamon
- 3 tbsp coconut oil

Method

Preheat your oven to 180c.

In a bowl combine the oats, orange zest, cranberries, honey, ginger, cinnamon, and coconut oil.

Spread out the granola mix on a baking tray lined with greaseproof paper and bake for 25 minutes. Give it a jiggle halfway through to ensure even cooking.

Tip

Let your granola air dry and cool after the oven before storing, this will prevent it getting soft.

Breakfast Bruschetta with Basil and Spinach Pesto

Prep time: 10 mins   Serves: 2

Tomatoes on bread will never not be utterly delicious. This refreshing breakfast always starts the day just right.

Ingredients

For the tomatoes:

- Large handful of cherry tomatoes, chopped
- 1 small red onion, finely diced
- 1 tsp olive oil
- 1 tsp balsamic vinegar

For the pesto:

- 2 tbsp olive oil
- Large bunch of fresh basil
- Handful of spinach
- 20g grated parmesan
- 3 tbsp pine nuts

For toast:

- 2 thick slices of sourdough
- 1 garlic clove

Method

In a bowl, mix together the tomato, onion, olive oil, and balsamic vinegar. Set aside.

To a blender, add the olive oil, basil, spinach, parmesan, and pine nuts. Blend until smooth.

Toast the sourdough and then rub each slice with the garlic clove. Now top your toast with the tomatoes and drizzle over the pesto.

Strawberry Baked Oats

Prep time: 5 mins   **Cooking time: 25 mins**   **Serves: 4**

This is a bit like having flapjacks for breakfast - needless to say, it is a spectacular way to start your day - it's deliciously filling and can be made in advance. A square of these baked oats is wonderful served warm from the oven, or even chilled from the fridge the next day.

Ingredients

- 1 large, ripe banana
- 1 egg
- 170ml oat milk
- 2 tbsp honey
- 130g rolled oats
- 1 tsp baking powder
- 2 large handfuls of strawberries, sliced

Method

Preheat your oven to 180c.

Grease and line a small baking dish (9x6 works well).

Begin by mashing the banana in a bowl and then adding the egg, oat milk, and honey. Give it a good mix until the ingredients are evenly combined.

Now stir in the oats, baking powder, and half of the strawberry slices.

Add the mix to your baking dish, flatten out the top, and then top with the rest of the strawberry slices.

Bake for 25 minutes until golden brown and crisp on top.

Spiced Apple and Raisin Bircher

Prep time: 5 mins   **Cooking time: 5 mins**   **Serves: 2**

I went through a phase of not being able to start my day without one of these. It's sweet, creamy, and filling. These really set you up to take on whatever the day throws at you. Serve them in jam jars so you can see those lovely layers!

Ingredients

- 75g oats
- 200ml apple juice
- 1 apple, peeled, cored, and diced.
- Handful of raisins
- ½ tsp cinnamon
- ½ tsp ground ginger
- 150g natural yoghurt

Method

To a bowl, add the oats and apple juice. Stir well and set aside to soak.

In a frying pan on medium heat, add a little olive oil and then the apple, raisins, cinnamon, and ginger. Add 50ml water and allow to cook for around 5 minutes until the water cooks off and the apple is soft.

Use some jam jars and fill the bottom with the oats. Top with natural yoghurt, and then top the Bircher muesli with the apple and raisin mix.

Enjoy these straight away or pop into the fridge for the next morning.

SOUPS

Ah - lovely, comforting soup – a steamy bowl of your favourite in rich, deep colours, accompanied by hot buttered toast has got to be one of life's greatest simple pleasures. I hope you find a new favourite in this flavour-packed collection.

Curried Parsnip Soup

Prep time: 10 mins   Cooking time: 35 mins   Serves: 4

This soup is thick, warm, and inviting. Team it with some crusty bread for dunking, and it's the perfect meal to warm your bones on a cold or rainy day.

Ingredients

- 500g parsnips, diced
- 2 tbsp olive oil
- 2 tsp curry powder
- 2 tsp garlic powder
- 1 tsp ground cumin
- 1 tsp ground coriander
- 1 tsp turmeric
- 1 red onion, sliced
- 2 garlic cloves, minced
- 900ml chicken stock
- 1/4 can of coconut milk

Method

Preheat your oven to 180c.

In a bowl, add the diced parsnip, olive oil, curry powder, garlic powder, ground cumin, ground coriander, and ground turmeric. Mix until evenly combined, and then spread out on a baking tray to roast in the oven for 30 minutes.

While the parsnips are roasting, add a little oil to a large pot and cook the sliced onion and minced garlic until soft. Add the chicken stock, and simmer on low heat until the parsnips are ready.

Once the parsnips are roasted, add these to the pot along with the coconut milk, and cook together for 5 minutes. Now blend the soup to your desired consistency, adding a little more water if required.

Serve your curried roast parsnip soup with hot buttered sourdough, and finish with a sprinkling of turmeric. Garnish with black pepper.

Pea and Asparagus Soup

Prep time: 5 mins   **Cooking time: 20 mins**   **Serves: 4**

Here's a vibrant looking soup to brighten up your day! Green is my favourite colour, and like this soup it always makes me happy.

Ingredients

- 1 bunch asparagus
- 500ml vegetable stock
- 200g peas
- 3 spring onions, sliced
- 1 garlic clove, minced
- Small bunch of mint, chopped
- Zest of half a lemon
- 2 tbsp natural yoghurt

Method

Preheat your oven to 180c.

Coat the asparagus in some olive oil, and then roast for 15 minutes.

While the asparagus is cooking, heat the vegetable stock in a pot on medium heat. Once it's boiling, add the peas, spring onions, garlic, and mint.

Lastly, add the roasted asparagus to the pot and blend. Stir through the lemon zest and yoghurt.

Tip:

Serving to friends and family? This soup looks lovely with a garnish of watercress piled in the centre. A real celebration of green!

Creamy Red Pepper and Basil Soup

Prep time: 5 mins **Cooking time: 30 mins** Serves: 2

These sweet and smoky roasted peppers paired with aromatic basil, are a flavour cornerstone of the soup world, and with good reason. This soup is good for the soul.

Ingredients

- 4 red peppers, diced
- 1 red onion, diced
- 3 garlic cloves, minced
- 1 tsp oregano
- 1 tbsp Worcestershire sauce
- 2 tbsp olive oil
- 400 ml vegetable stock
- 1 tbsp tomato puree
- Bunch of fresh basil leaves
- 3 tbsp creme fraiche

Method

Preheat your oven to 200c.

To a baking tray, add the peppers, onion, garlic, oregano, Worcestershire sauce, and olive oil. Give it a mix, and roast for 25 minutes until the veg is soft.

Remove from the oven and add to a blender with the vegetable stock, tomato puree, and basil leaves. Warm through and stir through the creme fraiche.

Dress with a basil leaf and a twist of black pepper.

Carrot and Ginger Soup

Prep time: 5 mins   Cooking time: 15 mins   Serves: 4

I think carrots need a strong partner to make a truly great soup. I love the kick of ginger in this soup. It has the ability to warm you on a cold day but wake you up on a mild one. Magic!

Ingredients

- 1 large onion, chopped
- 2 garlic cloves, minced
- 500g carrots, thinly sliced
- 2 inches of fresh ginger, peeled and grated
- ½ tsp turmeric
- 800ml vegetable stock

Method

Heat a little oil in a pan on low - medium heat. Add the onion and garlic, and fry until the onions have softened and turned golden brown. Add the carrots, ginger, turmeric, and vegetable stock.

Simmer for 10 minutes and then blend until smooth.

Creamy Spinach and Orzo Soup

Prep time: 5 mins   **Cooking time: 25 mins**   **Serves: 4**

Just heaven in a bowl! This is the most comforting dish, especially when served alongside cheese on toast.

Ingredients

- 1 white onion, sliced
- 2 garlic cloves, minced
- 2 tbsp plain flour
- 1 ltr vegetable stock
- 140g orzo
- 300g spinach, chopped
- 150g creme fraiche
- ½ tsp nutmeg
- Zest of half a lemon

Method

Heat a little oil in a pan on low - medium heat, then add the onion and garlic. Fry until the onions have softened and turned golden brown.

Now add the flour and stir until combined with the onions. Add vegetable stock, a little at a time.

Next mix in the orzo and cook for 10 minutes, stirring regularly, before adding the spinach, creme fraiche, nutmeg, and lemon zest. Cook for a further 5 minutes, or until the orzo is tender.

Serve and enjoy.

Spicy Sweet Potato Soup

Prep time: 10 mins   **Cooking time: 40 mins**   **Serves: 4**

This dish is naturally sweet, with a little warmth to keep your taste buds on its toes. It pairs well with a warm, crusty baguette.

Ingredients

- 6 medium size sweet potatoes, peeled and diced
- 3 tbsp olive oil
- 4 tbsp honey
- 2 garlic cloves, minced
- 1 tbsp thyme
- 1 tbsp chilli flakes
- 1 tsp smoked paprika
- 700ml vegetable stock
- 4 tbsp creme fraiche

Method

Preheat your oven to 180c.

Add to a baking tray the sweet potato, olive oil, honey, garlic, thyme, chilli flakes and smoked paprika. Mix the ingredients evenly then cover with foil and roast for 30 minutes, removing the foil halfway.

Once roasted, transfer the contents of the baking tray to a blender along with the vegetable stock and creme fraiche, and blend until smooth.

SALADS

"You don't make friends with salad," Marge Simpson sings in that one episode. And she's right; you don't... unless it's a good one. A good salad doesn't give leaves the centre stage. They add texture and notes of flavour sure, but the main characters are punchier, juicier, crunchier ingredients. A good salad defies the stereotype and is never boring. Never bland. I love plating up these colourful salads and bringing them to the table family-style. It's a real celebration of fresh, vibrant ingredients.

Cheese Crunch Lettuce Cups

Prep time: 10 mins   Serves: 2

Lettuce cups are incredibly versatile as starters for BBQ's, garden parties, as sides, or as lunch. Kids really love these too.

Ingredients

- 8 Baby Gem lettuce leaves
- 1 handful of cherry tomatoes, quartered
- 1 yellow pepper, diced
- ⅓ cucumber, diced
- 1 spring onion, finely sliced
- 60g extra mature Cheddar, grated
- 2 tbsp mayonnaise
- 1 tbsp natural yoghurt

Method

Break off the lettuce leaves, and wash and dry them.

In a bowl, add the tomatoes, peppers, cucumber, onion, grated Cheddar, mayonnaise, and natural yoghurt. Mix until evenly combined.

Spoon the cheese crunch mixture into the lettuce cups.

Goats Cheese and Apple Salad

Prep time: 5 mins   **Cooking time:** 3 mins   **Serves:** 4

For me, the best kind of salads are the ones where cheese is the main character. I love that tangy, creamy element against all the fresh and crunchy components. Goats cheese and apple are the best of friends, and this salad will happily see me through hot, cold, rain, or shine.

Ingredients

- 8 stems of asparagus, halved lengthways
- 1 bag of rocket
- 2 apples, cored, quartered, and thinly sliced.
- ½ red onion, thinly sliced
- 100g Goat cheese
- 3 tbsp olive oil
- 1 tbsp wholegrain mustard
- 1 tbsp honey
- Handful of walnuts, chopped

Method

Boil your asparagus in a pot for 2 minutes, then drain and run cold water over them to stop the cooking.

On a platter lay out a bed of rocket and spread over the apple slices, red onion, and asparagus. Crumble over the Goat cheese.

In a jug, mix together the olive oil, mustard, and honey. Season well and drizzle over the salad.

Toast the chopped walnuts in a pan on medium - high heat for 1 minute, and then sprinkle over to garnish.

Mango Couscous Salad

Prep time: 10 mins   **Serves: 2**

Sweet and zingy, this happy little salad works perfectly well all on its own, but also as a side dish.

Ingredients

- 80g couscous
- Juice of 1 lime
- An inch fresh grated ginger
- Handful of fresh flat leaf parsley, chopped
- 1 mango, diced
- 1 bag of rocket
- Handful of cashews

Method

Add the couscous to a bowl and cover with 200ml water. Leave to sit for 5 minutes until the water is absorbed, then add the lime juice, grated ginger, parsley, and stir.

Now stir through the mango, rocket, and cashews.

Avocado and Black Bean Chopped Salad

Prep time: 5 mins**Serves: 4**

This cool, creamy, and filling chopped salad is so versatile! It can be enjoyed on its own, over jacket potatoes, or even as a chunky salsa for tortillas.

Ingredients

- 1 avocado
- 1 red onion
- 4 lettuce leaves
- 2 handfuls of cherry tomatoes
- 1 tin of black beans
- 2 tbsp olive oil
- Juice of 1 lime
- 1 garlic clove, minced
- 1 bunch of fresh coriander

Method

Chop the avocado, onion, lettuce, and tomato into uniform-sized pieces, then add to a bowl along with the beans.

Stir through the olive oil, lime juice, garlic, and coriander.

Tip:

Choose avocados which are ripe, but still a little firm. Overripe avocados will be too mushy for this recipe.

Grilled Peaches with Burrata and Mint

Prep time: 5 mins   **Cooking time: 10 mins**   Serves: 4-6

This is a beautiful little dish to share with friends and family. It looks fantastic, and is perfect for everyone to sit around a table and enjoy, while digging in and catching up.

Ingredients

- 4 peaches, cut into wedges
- 1 tbsp olive oil
- 150g Burrata
- Small handful of mint, chopped
- Toasted ciabatta (optional)

Method

Remove the stones from your peaches and cut them into medium-sized wedges. You will get about 8 wedges per peach.

On medium heat, warm a griddle pan, while lightly brushing the peaches with olive oil. Add it to the grill, cooking for 4 - 5 minutes on each side, until you see lovely charred lines.

Once grilled, remove the peaches and arrange them on a round plate. In the centre, place the Burrata and dress the plate with a drizzle of olive oil, black pepper, and chopped mint.

This is great to serve with some toasted ciabatta slices. Just spread the burrata and grilled peaches onto it.

Tip:

Choose peaches which are ripe, but still quite firm. Over-ripe peaches will go mushy when grilled and can also burn easily due to the higher sugar content.

Chickpea Garden Salad with Honey Mustard Dressing

Prep time: 5 mins   Serves: 2

Chickpeas add a real satisfying texture to salads, not to mention they make them wonderfully filling. This salad is a real staple, and you can use it for fresh sides or for just about anything. Perfect for speedy weekday meals.

Ingredients

- 1 can of chickpeas, drained
- 1/2 Romaine lettuce, chopped
- 1/4 cucumber, quartered and chopped
- Large handful of cherry tomatoes, quartered
- 2 spring onions, finely sliced
- 40g mature Cheddar, cut into small cubes

For the dressing:

- 1 tbsp olive oil
- 1 tsp wholegrain mustard
- 1 tsp honey

Method

Add the chickpeas, lettuce, cucumber, tomatoes, spring onions, and Cheddar to a bowl, mixing it up. In a small jug whisk together the olive oil, wholegrain mustard, and honey. Now pour the mixture on top. Stir once more, and finish with some cracked black pepper.

Tip:

For extra texture, why not add a sprinkling of my roasted chickpeas from page 108.

Creamy Cucumber and Chinese Cabbage with Dill

Prep time: 5 mins   Serves: 4

A refreshing, crunchy salad with a delicious, creamy dill dressing. This makes a lovely side dish, but also works great as a slaw in burgers.

Ingredients

- 1 cucumber, deseeded and thinly sliced widthway
- 1 Chinese cabbage, thinly sliced
- 2 spring onions, finely chopped
- 3 tbsp natural yoghurt
- 1 tsp Dijon mustard
- 1 bunch fresh dill

Method

Well, this one couldn't be easier. Add all your ingredients to a bowl and mix to evenly combine.

Tip:

Keep your vegetables nice and thinly sliced. Use a mandolin or a very sharp knife.

Courgette and Lentil Salad with Caramelised Onions

Prep time: 10 mins   **Cooking time: 10 mins**   **Serves: 4**

This salad has lots of lovely, earthy flavours, so it is a great one to enjoy all year round.

Ingredients

- 1 tbsp butter
- 1 large white onion, finely sliced
- 1 tbsp balsamic vinegar
- 1 bag of mixed Italian leaves
- 1 courgette, grated
- 1 tin of green lentils

For the dressing:

- 2 tbsp olive oil
- 1 tbsp red wine vinegar
- 1 tbsp Dijon mustard

Method

Melt the butter in a frying pan, on medium heat. Once melted, add the onions and season well. Once softened add the balsamic vinegar and continue to cook until the onions are very soft and sticky. Set aside.

In a large serving bowl, layer the mixed leaves, lentils, and grated courgette. Top with the caramelised onions and then pour over the whisked dressing.

Greek Style Salad with Chunky Croutons

Prep time: 10 mins   Serves: 2

This is one of my all-time favourite salads, and this version adds a little more bite and texture with the addition of chunky toasted sourdough and a zingy dressing. Asymmetrical, odd chunks of tomato really work well with this dish to create visual interest and more texture.

Ingredients

- 2 beef tomatoes, cut into chunks
- ½ cucumber, deseeded and cut into chunks
- 1 red onion, thinly sliced
- ½ garlic clove, minced
- ½ tsp oregano
- 1 tbsp balsamic vinegar
- 2 thick slices sourdough, cut into large cubes
- 100g feta, crumbled

Method

Add the tomatoes, cucumber, red onion, garlic, and oregano to a bowl. Also add a large pinch of sea salt and lots of black pepper. Stir it up, and then add in the olive oil and balsamic vinegar.

Heat a frying pan on medium heat and lightly oil it, adding the sourdough cubes. Cook until it is toasted on all sides and has a nice crunch.

Stir the toasted croutons into the salad and serve with the feta crumbled on top. Finish with a final drizzle of olive oil and a twist of black pepper.

Tip:

Good tomatoes are key to the success of this dish. Ripen your tomatoes on a sunny windowsill until rich red and soft. They will be much sweeter after this.

Warm Kale, Sweet Potato and Apple Salad

Prep time: 5 mins   **Cooking time: 20 mins**   **Serves: 2**

I like to call this 'salad for non-salad weather'. When the thought of eating something cold completely turns you off, this lovely salad is warming, hearty, and filled with earthy flavours.

Ingredients

- 2 medium-sized sweet potatoes, peeled and diced
- 2 apples, peeled and sliced
- ½ tsp cinnamon
- ½ tsp smoked paprika
- 2 handfuls of kale, chopped
- 1 handful of pine nuts

Dressing:

- 2 tbsp olive oil
- 1 tsp Dijon mustard
- 1 garlic clove, minced
- 1 tsp rosemary

Method

Preheat your oven to 180c.

Add to a baking tray your kale, sweet potato, apple and pine nuts and coat in little olive oil. Then add the cinnamon and smoked paprika. Wrap in foil and roast for 20 minutes, or until soft.

Once cooked, add it to a bowl along with the dressing, then toss to combine the ingredients.

VEGGIES

Vegetable dishes can be so damn pretty, with all its beautiful textures and patterns. These dishes celebrate the savoury, and work to bring out those wonderful umami flavours. Whether you're a meat & two-veg, or meat-free and two-veg eater, these recipes make for some serious side dishes.

Charred Balsamic Sprouts

Prep time: 5 mins **Cooking time: 25 mins** **Serves: 4**

My relationship with sprouts has been turbulent. Love them or hate them, there's no denying that these tiny cabbages can be hard work. In my opinion, steamed sprouts can get tossed in the bin, but add a sweet infusion and some texture? That really makes them shine.

Ingredients

- 400g brussel sprouts, halved
- 4 sage leaves, finely chopped
- 3 tbsp olive oil
- 2 tbsp balsamic vinegar
- 2 tbsp honey

Method

Preheat your oven to 200c.

Add the brussel sprouts, sage, olive oil, balsamic vinegar, and honey to a baking tray. Season very generously, then mix to evenly coat the sprouts.

Roast for 25 minutes, or until the sprouts have developed some lovely, crispy browned bits.

Tip:

Try the spiced honey recipe at the end of this book - it works incredibly well with this dish!

Honey Miso Glazed Aubergines

Prep time: 5 mins   **Cooking time: 20 mins**   **Serves: 4**

Not only are these a breeze to make, but they are also really attractive, and I think it adds real interest to any dish that it accompanies. They look great served family-style, on a platter.

Ingredients

- 2 medium aubergines, halved
- 2 tbsp honey
- 1 tbsp miso paste
- 1 tbsp soy sauce
- 1 tbsp sesame oil
- 1 inch fresh ginger, peeled and grated
- 2 garlic cloves, minced

Method

Preheat your oven to 180c.

Score a criss-cross pattern in the flesh of the aubergine, and add to a baking tray, cut side up.

In a bowl, mix the miso paste, honey, soy sauce, sesame oil, ginger, and garlic to make a sauce. Use a brush to spread this over the aubergine flesh, using leftovers to coat the skin.

Roast for 20 minutes, or until golden brown, soft, and sticky.

Sesame Roasted Broccoli and Courgettes

Prep time: 5 mins   **Cooking time: 15 mins**   **Serves: 4**

This simple dish really enhances the savoury flavour of your greens. It's great as an everyday side dish to all kinds of meals, but how about trying this out for your next roast dinner as well?

Ingredients

- 300g tenderstem broccoli
- 1 large courgette, sliced diagonally into ovals
- 2 tbsp sesame oil
- 1 tbsp soy sauce
- 3 garlic cloves, minced
- 3 tbsp sesame seeds

Method

Preheat your oven to 200c.

To a baking tray, add your broccoli, courgette slices, and coat with the sesame oil, soy sauce, and minced garlic.

Roast for 15 minutes.

Tip:

Slice your courgette to about a 5mm thickness - very thin slices will go too soft in the oven.

Sticky Carrot and Courgette Ribbons

Prep time: 5 mins **Cooking time: 5 mins** Serves: 2

I adore veg with a sweet kick. This dish has some Asian inspired flavours, making it a fantastic fresh vegetable side, alongside rice and meats.

Ingredients

- 2 carrots, peeled into ribbons
- 2 courgettes, peeled into ribbons
- 2 garlic cloves, minced
- Juice of 1 clementine
- 1 tbsp honey
- 1 tbsp soy sauce
- 1 tbsp sesame seeds

Method

In a bowl add your carrot and courgette ribbons and coat in the garlic, clementine juice, honey, soy sauce, and sesame seeds.

Add a small amount of oil to a pan on medium-high heat, and fry the ribbons for 5 minutes until they wilt and develop a nice sticky glaze.

Tip:

When peeling the courgette, leave the seedy core. When your knife gets to the seedy part, turn the courgette to a fresh side to peel.

Creamy Minted Root Veg and Peas

Prep time: 5 mins   **Cooking time: 50 mins**   **Serves: 4**

We are cooking this all-in-one roasting tray for minimal washing up. This dish is both delicious and interesting enough to enjoy on its own, but it makes the perfect side to chicken and white fish. Why not try this out as a side for a Sunday roast?

Ingredients

- 2 parsnips, peeled and cut into chunks
- 2 carrots, peeled and cut into chunks
- 1 white onion, diced
- A few sprigs of fresh thyme
- 2 garlic cloves, minced
- 2 tbsp olive oil
- 120g peas
- 100ml creme fraiche
- 150ml milk
- 1 tsp Dijon mustard
- Handful of fresh mint leaves, finely chopped.

Method

Preheat your oven to 170c.

In a roasting tray add the parsnips, carrots, onion, thyme, garlic, and olive oil. Season well with salt and pepper, and then cover with foil and roast for 50 minutes, adding the peas after 40 minutes cooking time.

Remove from the oven, and stir through the creme fraiche, milk, Dijon mustard, and mint.

Kale with Caramelised Walnuts

Prep time: 5 mins   **Cooking time: 10 mins**   **Serves: 4**

Kale, but make it exciting. This dish is a real celebration of sweet and salty, which I love. The crunchy hit of sweet, caramelised walnuts adds an interesting dimension.

Ingredients

- 1 tbsp sesame oil
- 200g kale, chopped
- 1.5 tbsp soy sauce
- Large handful of walnuts, chopped
- 1 tsp butter
- 2 tbsp honey

Method

In a pan on medium heat, add the sesame oil. Once up to temperature, add in the kale and soy sauce. Now fry for 6 - 7 minutes, until tender.

Add your walnuts to a separate (dry) pan on medium heat, and let them toast a little. Move them around to prevent burning. Once they start smelling nice and nutty, add your butter and coat the walnuts. Next, add the honey and toss for 2 minutes. They will develop a lovely glaze.

Add the kale to a serving bowl, and top with the caramelised walnuts.

Spinach and Cauliflower Blue Cheese

Prep time: 5 mins **Cooking time: 25 mins** **Serves: 4**

Creamed spinach – good. Cauliflower cheese – good. But marry them together? Great! I love the rich hit of blue cheese with it too.

Ingredients

- 1 cauliflower, broken into florets
- 1 bag of spinach, chopped
- 2 tbsp butter
- 2 tbsp plain flour
- 400ml milk
- 3 garlic cloves, minced
- 1.5 tsp thyme
- 40g Stilton
- 40g mature Cheddar

Method

Preheat your oven to 200c.

Boil the cauliflower for 5 minutes. Meanwhile in a saucepan on low-medium heat, whisk together the butter and flour until a paste forms. Then add in the milk a little at a time, still whisking, until you have a sauce. Add the garlic, thyme, Stilton, and Cheddar, stirring until the cheese has melted.

Drain the cauliflower and add this to a dish along with the chopped spinach. Pour over the cheesy sauce and sprinkle the top with a little more Cheddar. Bake for 20 minutes.

Charred Corn with Smoked Paprika Butter

Prep time: 1 mins **Cooking time: 10 mins** Serves: 2

With just a little more effort, boiled sweetcorn can be transformed from a plain side to one with real attitude.

Ingredients

- 150g frozen sweetcorn
- 1 tsp olive oil
- 1 tbsp butter
- 1 tsp smoked paprika

Method

Add your frozen corn to a heat-proof jug and fill with boiling water. Let it steep for 1 minute and then drain.

Heat the olive oil in a pan on medium-high heat, then add the corn. Season well, and stir the corn intermittently, allowing it to char and develop dark patches. Cook until the corn has lots of blackened bits, then remove from the heat.

In your serving bowl mix the butter and smoked paprika, then season well. Add the corn and stir until the butter has melted.

LIGHT BITES

This section is perfect for when you are short of time. Being busy should not come at the sacrifice of being able to enjoy a tasty meal, so this section is full of dishes to delight your taste buds. There are ten-minute meals and recipes that need minimal prep time! So whipping these up for mid-week dinners will be easy.

Red Pepper and Basil Pasta

Prep time: 5 mins   **Cooking time: 10 mins**   **Serves: 2**

Incredibly simple and incredibly crowd pleasing, this is great for a mega speedy meal that all ages will love.

Ingredients

- 140g fusilli pasta
- 1 red onion thinly sliced
- 2 garlic cloves, minced
- 1 tbsp balsamic vinegar
- 1 red pepper, thinly sliced and cut into inch pieces.
- Handful of cherry tomatoes, sliced
- 1 tbsp tomato puree
- Handful of fresh basil
- Parmesan to finish.

Method

Add the pasta to a pot of boiling water.

While that's cooking, add a little olive oil to a pan on medium heat and cook the onion until soft. Then add the garlic and balsamic vinegar and cook together for a minute.

Now add the peppers, tomato, tomato purée, and ladle of water from the pasta. Allow to cook until the pasta is ready.

Drain the pasta and combine with the vegetable mix. Stir through the fresh basil, and serve with a grating of Parmesan on top.

Mediterranean Vegetable Tart

Prep time: 5 mins   **Cooking time: 25 mins**   **Serves: 4**

Another gloriously easy-to-prepare meal that still delivers big on flavour. I love this tart with a simple side salad, dressed with balsamic glaze.

Ingredients

- 1 sheet of puff pastry
- 1 red pepper, sliced
- 1 yellow pepper, sliced
- 1 red onion, sliced
- 2 garlic cloves, minced
- 1 tsp smoked paprika
- 1 tsp ground cumin
- 1 tsp oregano
- ½ tsp cinnamon
- Handful of tomatoes, halved
- 125g fresh Mozzarella, torn into small pieces
- 1 egg, beaten

Method

Preheat your oven to 200c.

In a pan on medium heat add a little oil. Then add the sliced peppers, onion, garlic, paprika, cumin, oregano, and cinnamon. Fry for 5 minutes.

Spread the vegetable mix evenly over the puff pastry sheet, leaving an inch border. Scatter over the tomatoes and Mozzarella.

Brush the border with the beaten egg and bake for 20 minutes.

Sweet Fried Plantain and Feta Tacos

Prep time: 20 mins   Cooking time: 15 mins   Serves: 2

Plantain is one of my favourite foods. Its natural sweetness is to die for, and it pairs unbelievably well with creamy, tangy feta. These tacos will have you doing the happy-food-dance.

Ingredients

- 120g masa harina
- 120ml warm water
- Pinch of salt
- 2 tbsp olive oil
- 1 large ripe plantain, sliced diagonally into oval slices
- Half a bag of rocket
- Small bunch of fresh coriander, chopped
- 40g feta

Method

First, we'll make the tortillas. Mix the masa harina and salt together in a bowl, then slowly mix in the water until a dough forms. Turn it out onto a clean surface and knead for 5 - 10 minutes, until smooth. Cornmeal does not create an elastic dough like wheat flour, but kneading allows the moisture to be absorbed. Rest the dough for 10 minutes.

Cut the dough into 6 portions and roll into thin circles. Heat a pan on very high heat. When very hot, add tortillas to the pan, one at a time, without any oil, and cook for 40 - 60 seconds on each side. It will develop brown spots when it is sufficiently cooked. Keep your cooked tortillas warm in the oven, at about 50c.

Add the oil to the pan on medium heat and fry the plantain for 60 - 90 seconds on each side, until it is caramelised and soft.

Build your tortillas! Add a layer of rocket, then pile on the fried plantain, crumble over the feta, and a sprinkle of coriander. (Try the spiced honey at the end of this book, it tastes amazing on these tacos!)

Tip:

When I was younger, I could never get my plantain right, so I turned to my mother-in-law for advice. Turns out what I thought was a ripe plantain, was not. She told me, "When it looks really quite black, and like it might be ready for the compost bin, then it's ready!"

Creamy Spinach Stuffed Mushrooms

Prep time: 10 mins **Cooking time: 20 mins** **Serves: 4**

Whether you're having it as a light bite or a side dish - however you prefer, just make sure that you eat it. It. Is. Good.

Ingredients

- 4 large flat mushrooms
- 2 tbsp olive oil
- Large handful of spinach, finely chopped
- 100g Mascarpone
- 1 tsp balsamic vinegar
- 3 garlic cloves, minced
- 1 tbsp fresh rosemary, finely chopped
- Handful of grated Parmesan

Method

Preheat your oven to 180c.

Remove the stems from your mushrooms. Brush the outside of each mushroom with olive oil.

To a bowl, add the finely chopped spinach, Mascarpone, balsamic vinegar, garlic, and rosemary. Season and mix well.

Using a spoon, add the mix generously to the inside of your mushrooms and then dip the top of each stuffed mushroom in the grated Parmesan.

Add the mushrooms to a baking tray and bake.

Couscous with Slow Roasted Tomatoes and Parmesan

Prep time: 5 mins   **Cooking time: 40 mins**   **Serves: 4**

Couscous is so chewy and satisfying to eat - especially flavoured with sweet, slow-roasted tomatoes, and a salty hit of Parmesan.

Ingredients

- 120g masa harina
- 120ml warm water
- Pinch of salt
- 2 tbsp olive oil
- 1 large ripe plantain, sliced diagonally into oval slices
- Half a bag of rocket
- Small bunch of fresh coriander, chopped
- 40g feta

Method

Preheat your oven to 150c.

To a baking tray, add the tomatoes, olive oil, balsamic vinegar, oregano, and garlic. Mix well then lay the tomatoes, cut side facing up. Roast for 40 minutes.

Add the couscous to a bowl and cover with the boiled vegetable stock. Leave to sit for 5 minutes until the water is absorbed. Season generously and add the lemon zest.

Stir through the roasted tomatoes and Parmesan shavings.

Cavolo Nero Spaghetti with Garlic and Lemon

Prep time: 5 mins   **Cooking time: 10 mins**   **Serves: 2**

This is such a quick and easy dinner. It is perfect for evenings when you are short of time, but short of time doesn't necessarily mean we need to compromise on flavour. No, no, no - this simple dish will have your taste buds rejoicing.

Ingredients

- 200g spaghetti
- 2 large handfuls of sliced cavolo nero
- 4 garlic cloves, minced
- A few sprigs of fresh thyme, stemmed
- Juice of half a lemon
- 30g Parmesan

Method

Add your spaghetti to boiling water and cook to your liking.

While the spaghetti is cooking, add a little olive oil to a pan on medium heat, then add the cavolo nero, garlic, thyme, and lemon juice.

Drain the spaghetti and add to the pan with the cavolo nero. Grate in the Parmesan, then stir through and serve.

Roasted Vegetable Orzo

Prep time: 5 mins **Cooking time: 35 mins** **Serves: 4**

My infatuation with orzo is no secret. This stuff is delicious and adds a nice chewy bite, especially alongside roasted vegetables. Here we cook the orzo in vegetable stock, so it soaks up all that good flavour. This meal is packed with goodness and wonderfully hearty too.

Ingredients

- 1 aubergine, diced
- 1 red onion, diced
- 1 red pepper, diced
- 100g vine ripened tomatoes, halved
- 4 garlic cloves, minced
- 2 tbsp olive oil
- 1 tbsp Worcestershire sauce
- 1 tsp oregano
- 1 tsp cumin
- 1 tsp sumac
- 100g orzo
- 700ml vegetable stock
- 40g feta
- Small handful of fresh parsley, chopped

Method

Preheat your oven to 160c.

Add the aubergine, onion, pepper, and tomatoes to a tray and coat with the olive oil, garlic, Worcestershire sauce, oregano, cumin, and sumac. Season with salt and pepper, then stir to combine. Roast for 20 minutes, stirring halfway through.

In a pan, add the orzo and vegetable stock and cook on medium heat for 15 minutes. Once the orzo is cooked and the liquid has cooked off, add the vegetables and stir to combine.

Crumble in the feta and sprinkle over the parsley. Serve.

Broccoli Pasta

Prep time: 5 mins **Cooking time: 10 mins** **Serves: 2**

It all started when I began making this regularly as a meal for my baby. It was very quick, needed minimal ingredients, and was a lovely, nutritious meal. "I should be making this for us," I said to my husband… and here we are! It's so quick and tasty that you'll wonder why you never made it before.

Method
Ingredients

- 150g wholewheat pasta
- 2 large handfuls of frozen or fresh broccoli florets
- 1 tbsp olive oil
- 1 garlic clove, minced
- 1 tsp mixed herbs
- 20g parmesan

In a pot with salted, boiling water, add the pasta and cook to your liking.

In a separate pot, boil the broccoli until soft enough to mash it with a fork without it being completely mushy.

Once the broccoli is cooked, drain the water and mash it.

Drain the cooked pasta and return to the pot along with the broccoli olive oil, minced garlic, mixed herbs, and stir well. Grate in the parmesan and stir. Serve with a little more parmesan on top.

Courgette Fritters with Lemon Yoghurt

Prep time: 10 mins   Cooking time: 8 mins   Serves: 8

Whether you are nine or ninety, you are going to absolutely love these. Make a batch in advance of the week ahead and you've got yourself an fabulous snack, ready to go.

Method

Ingredients

For the fritters:

- 1 medium courgette, grated
- 30g feta cheese
- Handful of fresh dill, finely chopped
- 1 tsp garlic powder
- 1 large egg
- 3 tbsp plain flour

For the lemon yoghurt:

- 6 tbsp natural yoghurt
- 1 lemon
- 1 garlic clove, minced

To a bowl, add the grated courgette, feta, dill, garlic powder, and egg. Season well and stir together, then sprinkle in the flour and mix until evenly combined.

Using clean hands, form the fritters into six patties. Oil a frying pan on medium heat and cook the fritters two at a time for 1 minute each side, or until they are crisp on the outside and nicely browned.

To make the dip, add to the natural yoghurt, the minced garlic, zest of 1 lemon, and half the juice. Season and serve alongside the fritters.

Tip:

Courgettes can sometimes hold a lot of water which you'll want to get rid of to prevent soggy fritters. Wrap the grated courgette in a kitchen towel or a clean tea towel, and squeeze the water out.

SNACKS

Feeling peckish? Here you will find some handy batch recipes to keep you covered for a good, few snacks. There are lots of fruit and veg-filled options, and most importantly - they're filling. Nothing worse than a snack that doesn't touch the sides, am I right?

Pear and Ginger Cakes

Prep time: 10 mins   Cooking time: 20 mins   Serves: 12

Pears are a seriously underrated fruit, in my opinion. I just adore them! These lovely little cakes are naturally sweet and guaranteed to make your next tea break a joy.

Ingredients

- 140g unsalted butter, room temperature
- 3 tbsp honey
- 1 tsp vanilla extract
- 2 eggs
- 100g self-raising flour
- 100g ground almonds
- 2 tsp ground ginger
- 1 tsp baking powder
- pinch of salt
- 2 medium sized pears, peeled and finely diced

Method

Preheat your oven to 160c.

In a bowl, whisk together the butter, honey, vanilla, and eggs. Once combined, add the flour, ground almonds, ginger, baking powder, and salt. Fold in using a wooden spoon.

Once you have a smooth cake batter, add the pears and fold once more.

Spoon into cake cases and bake for 20 minutes, or until a toothpick pricked into the centre of a cake comes out clean.

Tip:

Avoid using over-ripe pears which will be too mushy and juicy for this recipe.

Date and Cashew Bars

Prep time: 10 mins + 30 mins chilling   **Serves:** 8

I think these bars are such a joy to add to packed lunches. They're sweet, sticky, and made with love… not to mention a lot cheaper and more wholesome than store-bought versions.

Ingredients

- 100g dates
- 60g cashews
- 40g raisins
- Zest of 1 orange

Method

Add all the ingredients to a blender and blitz until the fruit and nuts are very small, something close to a sticky, gritty consistency.

Remove from the blender and place onto some greaseproof paper, now form into a ball. Wrap this up and chill in the fridge for 30 minutes.

Once chilled, add another layer on top of the ball and roll the mixture into a thick rectangle - about as thick as your thumb.

Use a large knife to cut bar portions. Individually wrap the bars in greaseproof paper and store in the fridge, ready for lunches.

Sweet and Spicy Roasted Chickpeas

Prep time: 2 mins **Cooking time: 20 mins** **Serves: 6**

These roasted chickpeas have a lovely light crunch and are great to make in advance of feeling snacky. They also work as a delicious alternative to croutons in salads.

Ingredients

- 1 tin of chickpeas
- 1 tbsp olive oil
- 1 tbsp ground cumin
- 1 tbsp curry powder
- 1 tbsp castor sugar

Method

Preheat your oven to 170c.

Drain the chickpeas and dry them off using a paper towel or a tea towel. Add them to a bowl with the olive oil, cumin, curry powder, and sugar, then stir until the chickpeas are evenly coated.

Tip the chickpeas onto a baking tray and give them a shake to ensure they are evenly spread out.

Roast for 20 minutes, giving it another shake halfway through.

Store in an airtight container to maintain its delicate crunch.

Courgette Scones

Prep time: 10 mins   Cooking time: 15 mins   Serves: 12

Courgette scones have a lovely, subtle, earthy flavour, which tastes wonderful with some salted butter.

Ingredients

- 220g self-raising flour
- 1 tsp baking powder
- 1 tbsp oregano
- 50g cold butter, cubed
- 150g mature Cheddar, grated
- 1 courgette, grated and drained
- 150ml milk

Method

Preheat your oven to 200c.

In a bowl, add the flour, baking powder, oregano, and cubed butter. Rub the butter and flour mixture together with your fingertips until a crumb is formed. You're done when the crumb is even, and you have no large chunks of butter left.

Now add the grated courgette and grated Cheddar (keep a little to sprinkle on top later), then mix until evenly combined. Stir in the milk until a dough has formed, and turn it out onto a clean, floured surface.

Knead the dough until it comes together to form a moist but firm dough. Then roll it out to 2cm thick. Use your cutter to cut out the scone shapes and place it onto a lined baking tray. Brush the top of your scones with some milk, then sprinkle over some more grated cheese.

Bake for 15 minutes, or until golden brown with a bubbly cheesy topping.

Tip:

Courgettes can hold lots of moisture, which we don't want in the scone mix. So once grated, wrap in a clean tea towel, and give it a squeeze to drain out the excess moisture.

Rustic Oatcakes

Prep time: 10 mins   Cooking time: 20 mins   Serves: 12

You know me, I love rustic. Oatcakes especially, always make me feel cosy and old fashioned. They are very easy to make and perfect for keeping hunger at bay between meals. I love mine slathered with herby cream cheese.

Ingredients

- 170g oats
- 40g wholemeal flour
- Pinch of salt
- ¼ tsp bicarbonate of soda
- 50g cold butter, cubed

Method

Preheat your oven to 170c.

In a bowl, mix the oats, flour, salt, bicarbonate of soda, and butter. With clean hands, rub together the mixture between your fingers until a consistent crumb forms.

Pour in 50ml hot water a little at a time until a dough forms. It will be thick!

Dust a clean work surface with flour and roll out the dough to about 5mm. Use a large cookie cutter to stamp out your oatcakes. (Repeat the process with the trimmings).

Place the oatcakes onto a baking tray, lined with greaseproof paper, and bake for 20 minutes. They will be lightly golden.

Allow to cool before serving.

Carrot and Orange Loaf

Prep time: 10 mins   Cooking time: 45 mins   Serves: 8

I will take a rustic recipe like this over a chocolate cake any day! This is perfect to make ahead of the week, so you have something sweet and satisfying ready to enjoy.

Ingredients

- 2 large eggs
- 100ml olive oil
- Zest and juice of 1 orange
- 80ml honey
- 1 tsp vanilla extract
- 1 large carrot, finely grated
- 300g self-raising flour
- 1 tsp baking powder
- 1 tsp cinnamon
- 1 tsp ground ginger
- Pinch of salt

Method

Preheat your oven to 180c. Line an 8x4 inch loaf pan with greaseproof paper.

In a bowl, whisk together the eggs, oil, orange juice, zest, honey, and vanilla. Then gently stir in the grated carrot.

Now add the flour, baking powder, cinnamon, ginger, and salt. Gently fold in with your wooden spoon until combined. Avoid over-mixing.

Pour the batter into the loaf pan and bake for 45 minutes, or until a toothpick pricked into the loaf comes out clean.

Tip:

If you would like a sweeter loaf, mix 2 tablespoons of marmalade with a splash of water to loosen it up, then use a brush to glaze the top of the loaf.

Creamy Spinach Pinwheels

Prep time: 10 mins **Cooking time: 15 mins** **Serves: 14**

The mix in these pinwheels is very similar to the filling of a delicious ravioli that I often make (the recipe is in my first cookbook). I like it so much that I found more than one way to enjoy it.

Ingredients

- 200g spinach, finely chopped
- 2 garlic cloves, minced
- 125g Mascarpone
- 50g Parmesan
- ½ tsp nutmeg
- Zest of 1 lemon
- 1 sheet puff pastry
- 1 egg, beaten

Method

Preheat your oven to 170c.

In a bowl mix together the spinach, garlic, Mascarpone, Parmesan, nutmeg, and lemon zest.

Spread the mixture out evenly across the puff pastry sheet. Now roll the sheet lengthways into a sausage shape, and cut into 2cm thick slices.

Place the slices on a baking tray and brush with beaten egg. Bake for 15 minutes.

DIPS AND DRESSINGS

The sauce *maketh'* the meal. Personally, I love a condiment, and prefer my food slathered in saucy goodness. These dips and dressings will elevate your snacks and salads to god-tier level.

Garlic Sauce

Prep time: 5 mins   Cooking time: 30 mins   Serves: 4

Homemade garlic sauce couldn't be easier, and it is absolutely packed with flavour. Make up a batch for the week and have it with everything. Roasting the garlic adds depth of flavour and removes the fiery hum that might otherwise linger on your tastebuds for the rest of the day.

Ingredients

- 8 garlic cloves, peeled
- 1 tbsp olive oil
- 6 tbsp natural yoghurt
- Juice of half a lemon

Method

Preheat your oven to 180c.

Add the peeled garlic cloves to some foil and coat evenly with olive oil. Season and wrap the foil, (leaving some space for air to circulate), then roast for 30 minutes.

Once roasted, add the garlic cloves to a bowl and mash with a fork until a paste forms. Now add the natural yoghurt, lemon juice, and season generously with plenty of black pepper.

Green Sauce

Prep time: 5 mins   Serves: 4

This sauce adds a burst of happiness to your plate with its glorious, vibrant green shade! I love to blend it to a smooth consistency and enjoy with chicken or fish, and potatoes. It's great as a light sauce for ravioli too.

Ingredients

- 50ml olive oil
- 1 tsp Dijon mustard
- Large handful of flat-leaf parsley
- 6 garlic cloves
- 2 tbsp capers
- Zest of 1 lemon

Method

Simply add all the ingredients to a blender, season well, and blend until the sauce is smooth.

Sweet Garlic and Thyme Dressing

Prep time: 5 mins　　**Serves:** 4

A celebration of familiar, earthy flavours. Perfect with warm salads, potatoes, and roasted veggies. I love this as an alternative to butter on a jacket potato!

Ingredients

- 100ml olive oil
- 2 tbsp red wine vinegar
- 1 garlic clove, minced
- A few sprigs of fresh thyme

Method

Add the olive oil, red wine vinegar, and minced garlic to a bowl or a jug. Remove the thyme leaves from the stems and add these to the dressing. Season well, and whisk until thoroughly combined.

Serve immediately.

The Perfect Guac

Prep time: 5 mins　　**Serves:** 4

I will eat guacamole not only as a dip, but as a side with pretty much anything. Whether it's dolloped over a salad, served with crispy fried fish, spread on a sandwich… I absolutely love the stuff. Of course, guacamole also works wonderfully as a fresh dip for your tortillas and vegetable crudites. I add Worcestershire sauce for a surprise zing!

Ingredients

- 2 large hass avocado (soft)
- 1 red onion, very finely diced
- 2 garlic cloves, minced
- Juice of a lime
- Handful of fresh coriander, chopped
- Dash of Worcestershire sauce

Method

Scoop the avocados into a bowl and mash it with a fork. Keep some texture in the avocado by not making it a smooth paste.

Mix in the red onion, garlic, lime juice, coriander, and Worcestershire sauce. Mix to combine.

Tip:

Guacamole looks best served straight after preparing, while it still has that lovely green of the avocado before it oxidises. As well as adding flavour, the lime juice will help prevent browning, but you can also slow browning by placing clingfilm over the surface of the guacamole to stop it from coming into contact with air.

Sweet Onion Dip

Prep time: 5 mins   **Cooking time: 15 mins**   **Serves: 4**

I adore onion dip, and it couldn't be easier to make it at home. It's perfect with vegetable crudites, breadsticks, tortilla chips… anything really!

Ingredients

- 2 tbsp rapeseed oil
- 2 large white onions, thinly sliced
- 3 garlic cloves, minced
- 1 tbsp balsamic vinegar
- 200g Greek yoghurt
- Handful of fresh chives

Method

In a pan on low - medium heat, add the oil and the onions. Once the onions are soft, add the garlic and balsamic vinegar and season well.

Keep cooking the onions, stirring regularly, until they are a rich brown and very soft. Now add the onions to a blender with the Greek yoghurt and chives and blend until smooth.

Tip:

Garlic burns very easily, it's best to add it to your cooking after the onions. This way it gets protected from the heat.

Whipped Feta with Spiced Chickpeas

Prep time: 5 mins   **Cooking time: 20 mins**   **Serves: 4**

This dip is packed with flavour, and it looks marvellous too. Load it onto your tortillas at your next film night!

Ingredients

- ½ can of chickpeas, drained
- 1 tbsp olive oil
- 1 tsp cumin
- 1 tsp garlic powder
- 300g Greek yoghurt
- 100g feta
- 1 garlic clove, minced
- Zest of 1 lemon

Method

Preheat your oven to 170c.

Add the chickpeas to a roasting tray and coat them with the olive oil, cumin, and garlic powder. Season well. Roast for 20 minutes, giving them a jiggle halfway through.

To a food processor, (or you can hand whip this too!), add the Greek yoghurt, feta, garlic, and lemon zest. Blitz or hand whisk until you have a light and fluffy consistency.

Spread the whipped feta in a dish and top with the roasted chickpeas.

Peanut Dressing

Prep time: 5 mins   Serves: 4

I'm going to appease both sides of the peanut butter coin by saying that you can use whichever texture you feel passionately about (I know you feel passionately about it)! I am team smooth. Forever. I will die here. Anyway, enjoy this delicious dressing. It's wonderful on crunchy lettuce and cucumber!

Ingredients

- 2 tbsp peanut butter
- 2 tbsp natural yoghurt
- 1 clove garlic, minced
- 1 tsp ginger paste
- 1 tbsp honey
- 2 tbsp water

Method

Warm up your peanut butter either in the microwave or on the hob, until it is runny. Add this to a bowl with the natural yoghurt, garlic, ginger paste, and honey. Whisk together until it is light and aerated.

Tip:

If you do love some crunch, then finish your salad with a sprinkle of chopped, salted peanuts for some added texture.

Spiced Honey

Prep time: 5 mins   Cooking time: 5 mins   Serves: 24

I wish I had brought this into my life sooner because it is game changing! Put it on anything… breakfast, tacos, salads, vegetables… you name it, everything is elevated with this in your kitchen.

Ingredients

- 340g clear honey
- 5 red chillies, sliced
- 1 tbsp chilli flakes
- Small bunch of thyme

Method

Add your honey, chilies, chilli flakes, and thyme to a saucepan and warm on low - medium heat, until it comes to a gentle boil.

Let this cook for 5 minutes, stirring regularly.

Remove from the heat and once cooled, pour the honey through a sieve into an airtight jar.

Discard the chillies and thyme.

Once completely cool, close your airtight jar.

Tip:

How spicy your honey will be, comes down to your choice of chillies, and whether you keep the seeds in it or not. Adjust to your desired heat level.

Ginger, Honey and Lime Dressing

Prep time: 5 mins   Serves: 4

This dressing is perfect for any salad that you want to add a zingy, lively note to. It works with all meats, fruits, veggies… a very versatile dressing to have in your culinary arsenal.

Ingredients

- 100ml olive oil
- 1 tbsp freshly grated ginger
- 2 tbsp honey
- 1 lime (zest and juice)

Method

Add all the ingredients to a bowl or a jug. Using a fork or a hand whisk, mix the ingredients together until thoroughly combined. Serve immediately over your salad or meal of choice.

Tip:

Limes can be reluctant to give up the juice. Roll them back and forth on your kitchen counter, quite hard, before cutting them open. This will get a lot more juice out of them.

Thank You

My husband:
My wonderful partner in food. Love of my life! Thank you for patiently waiting to eat your lukewarm dinner that I have spent an age photographing. Thank you for eating the bloopers. Thank you for being the most fun person to enjoy a meal with. You always keep me excited for the future because the past and present has been so incredible.

My son:
It won't be long until you are able to chomp your way through all the recipes in this book. You can give most of them a good go! My little food lover in the making, and my biggest source of inspiration. I will continue to push myself out of my comfort zone for you.

My family:
Thank you, Mum and Dad - for being such adorable promoters - telling every neighbour, shop owner, and passer-by who will listen, where they can get their copy of my book. I feel very lucky to have such wonderful parents who taught me the joys of cooking from such an early age. That luck doubles in being blessed with such lovely, supportive in-laws as well.

The community:
The online 'Girl Eats World' community has been nothing short of amazing, and nothing gives me more of a buzz than seeing you share the recipes you have made. I like to think that over the years we have built a wonderfully fun online network of like-minded food enthusiasts, who are always keen to learn and try new things.

Kingsley Publishers:
One summer's day in 2021 I was sat in my garden, 9 months pregnant and ready to pop. I was feeling dejected after a year-long search for a publisher - when suddenly an email appears in my inbox… showing interest and wanting to chat further. It was the beginning of the journey, and what an exciting journey it has been! Thank you, Kingsley, for taking a chance on this unknown author and making it all happen.

About the Author

Jo is a food writer from Bedford, where she lives with husband Alex, son Callum, and Kimchi the cat. In 2012, Jo founded her food blog to share recipes, food experiences, and travel stories. Over time *GirlEatsWorld.co.uk* grew into a hub for recipe inspiration, drawing an enthusiastic, fellow-food-loving community.

In 2021, Jo published her debut cookbook *'Cook It, Eat It, Live It',* which was a well-received personal collection of recipes from her home, and an ethos on finding joy in everyday life through food. Jo continues to be passionate about the everyday joy of food, celebrated in hearty, wholesome cooking.

If you love to cook and eat, then join the online community! You can find more recipes at *GirlEatsWorld.co.uk,* and you can follow Jo on all social media at *@jogirleatsworld* or say hello at *jo@girleatsworld.co.uk.*

COOK IT, EAT IT LIVE IT

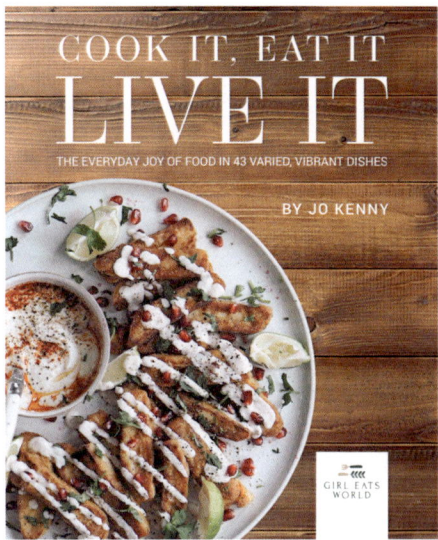

Cook it Eat it Live it is written by Jo Kenny, food writer and owner of GirlEatsWorld.co.uk.

In this first publication, Jo offers readers a vibrant and varied collection of recipes inspired by both travel and family ties to the UK, Japan, Guyana, the Caribbean.

This delicious collection of every day recipes satisfies appetites for light bites, indulgent dinners, fresh sides and delicious desserts.You'll find a spectrum of dishes from rich, earthy flavours to fresh aromatics giving you meals to enjoy year round. All recipes are firm favourites in Jo's own household and cooked regularly. This is family style, everyday inspiration to ensure no more boring dinners.

Inside *Cook it Eat it Live it*, you'll find recipes the whole family will enjoy, such as:

- Jo's Signature Lamb Stew with Sage Dumplings
- Creamy Chicken and Smoked Bacon Stew with Cheesy Mash
- Spinach Ravioli with Lemon and Sage Butter
- Mac and Cheese with Caramelised Onion and Bacon Crumb
- Tamarind Duck with Rice
- Creamy Lamb and Potato Curry
- Spatchcock Chicken with Spring Onions and Clementines
- Charred Pineapple Salsa
- Mango and Lime Cream Pudding
- Fudgy Banana Brownies

Recipes are punctuated with stories of travel, food inspirations and a personal philosophy of enjoying food unapologetically. **Cook it Eat it Live it** is about finding happiness in the little things and injecting some joy into every day life through wholesome, exciting meals.

Jo's Signature Lamb Stew with Sage Dumplings

Prep time: 35 mins   Cooking time: 55 mins   Serves: 4-6

This is a personal favourite. I created this recipe many years ago, and it will be the one that I pass down through generations. This dish fills me with complete joy. The meat is tender, the sauce is sweet and earthy, and let's not forget those delicious, comforting sage dumplings. The moment the seasons change and it becomes darker and colder outdoors, this is my go-to recipe. Enjoy!

Equipment

- bowl
- knife
- chopping board
- garlic press
- large Dutch oven or pot with a lid.
- wooden spoon

Ingredients

For the dumplings:

- 250g self raising flour
- 120g cold butter, cubed
- handful of fresh sage leaves, finely chopped

For the stew:

- knob of salted butter
- a few sprigs of fresh thyme, finely chopped
- 1 large white onion, diced
- 1 tbsp balsamic vinegar
- 3 garlic cloves, minced
- 4-6 lamb chops (bone on)
- 1/2 tube tomato puree
- 1 tbsp wholegrain mustard
- 1 courgette, thickly diced
- large handful of fresh plum tomatoes, halved
- 1 tin chopped tomatoes

Method

Preheat your oven to 180c.

First get the dumplings ready:

In a bowl rub together the flour and butter until you have a crumb-like mixture. Mix in the chopped sage and season well. Add cold water, one tablespoon at a time, and mix until a thick dough forms. Note that you won't need much water! Set aside and turn your attention to stew making...

Melt your butter with seasoning and thyme, in a large pot, on medium heat. Once heated add the diced onion and cook until soft. Add the balsamic to deglaze the pan and make the onions sweet. Add the minced garlic. Place in the lamb chops and allow them to brown on each side. Now add in the tomato purée and mustard. Stir until coated. Add the courgette, fresh tomatoes, and tinned chopped tomatoes. Stir well but carefully, so as not to break the meat. Allow to cook until the liquid has reduced and thickened.

Roll the dumpling dough into 8-10 large, thick ovals, and place in a ring around the edge of the stew. Give them a gentle press, so half of the dumpling sits in the sauce. Now cover with a lid and cook in the oven for 15 minutes. Remove the lid and bake for a further 5-10 minutes, until the dumplings are lightly golden and crisp on top.

I recommend serving with rice to soak up all that lovely tomato sauce.

Tip

If you're entertaining with this dish, make the stew the night before. The flavours will develop overnight and it'll taste even more amazing the next day. Simply bring the stew to room temperature, then top with dumplings the day of serving and cook for 15-20 minutes, uncovered at 180c.

Creamy Chicken and Smoked Bacon Stew with Cheesy Mash

Prep time: 10 mins   Cooking time: 35 mins   Serves: 6

This is the kind of dinner you make after a cold day that chilled you to the bones. The flavours in this one-pot delight are made up of familiar favourites. I always imagine eating this meal by candlelight.

Equipment

- large pot
- colander
- large Dutch oven pot
- knife
- chopping board
- garlic press
- wooden spoon
- measuring jug
- box grater
- potato masher

Ingredients

For the stew:

- 1 large white onion, diced
- 4 cloves of garlic, minced
- 2 tbsp Worcestershire sauce
- 4 chicken breasts, diced
- handful fresh thyme, finely chopped
- 2 tsp dried mixed herbs
- 200g smoked bacon lardons
- large handful of asparagus, cut into inch-long pieces
- 1 cup peas (fresh or frozen)
- 1.5 tbsp plain flour
- 200ml chicken stock
- 300ml creme fraiche

For the mash topping:

- 6 medium-large Maris Piper potatoes, cut into inch-chunks (skins on)
- 1 tbsp butter
- 100g extra strong cheddar, grated

Method

Preheat your oven to 200c. Add the potatoes to a pot of boiling water and allow it to cook for around 10-12 minutes or until soft, while you make the stew.

Add the pot to the hob on medium heat, and warm a little oil. Add the diced onions and allow it to soften for a few minutes, before adding the garlic and Worcestershire sauce. Cook for another 1-2 minutes until caramelised and golden brown.

Add the chicken breast and season generously. Stir continuously for a few minutes to cook the outside of the chicken evenly. Add the chopped thyme, mixed herbs, and bacon lardons. Stir for another 2-3 minutes then add the asparagus and peas. Add in the flour and stir well before adding the chicken stock. Allow to cook together for a further 5 minutes, before adding the creme fraiche. Stir well and reduce the heat to the lowest setting.

Now it's time to focus on the mash.

Drain the water from your potatoes and return to the pot it cooked in. Season generously, add butter and get to mashing. Once smooth, add your grated cheddar and mash once more. Remove the stew from heat and spoon mash on top. Once evenly covered, use a fork to create texture in the potato. This is how you get those delicious crispy bits. Add a little more grated cheese if desired (I mean why not), and cook pot (without lid) in the oven for 15 minutes.

Chipolata and Mushroom Stew with Mustard Mash

Prep time: 10 mins   **Cooking time:** 30 mins   **Serves:** 4

If you're looking for a mid-week comfort, or an easy weekend meal, either way this is a great staple for hearty home cooking. It gives a nod to good ol' sausage and mash then throws in a little extra pizzazz!

Equipment

- frying pan
- knife
- chopping board
- garlic Press
- 2 large pots
- wooden spoon
- measuring jug
- peeler
- colander
- potato masher

Ingredients

For the stew:

- 12 chipolatas
- 1 red onion, diced
- 4 garlic cloves, minced
- 1 pack of shiitake mushrooms, sliced
- handful of fresh rosemary, chopped
- 1 tbsp Worcestershire sauce
- 1 cup frozen peas
- 2 tbsp plain flour
- 200ml chicken stock
- 200ml milk

For the mash:

- 4-5 large Maris Piper potatoes
- 1 large knob of butter
- 1 tbsp wholegrain mustard

Method

In a frying pan, fry your chipolatas on medium heat with a little oil, until nicely browned. Once cooked remove from heat and set aside.

In a large pot, heat up some rapeseed oil and add the red onion. Once softened add the garlic, mushrooms, and rosemary. Once the mushrooms are softened, add the Worcestershire sauce and peas. When the peas soften, stir in flour a little at a time until all the ingredients are evenly coated and very thick. Now add chicken stock a little at a time, and keep stirring. Next, slowly add the milk and a delicious creamy sauce will form.

Simmer on low heat until the mixture is reduced to a rich and thick sauce. Add chipolatas to the stew and heat through once more.

Peel and dice potatoes into 2 inch thick chunks and boil for 10 minutes. Mash with butter and mustard, and season well.